MW01537073

Oren's Gift

A Poem of Hope

Written by **Joanne Fortino**

Illustrated by **Michael and Joanne Fortino**

For our two wonderful and amazing children, Juliana and Evan…and to all parents who wish they had a "magical blanket" to make the world the best it can be for their children.

1

Good morning to you and
good morning to all!

Today I have noticed that
I've grown quite tall.

Rather grand and quite lofty,
a strong young boy,

who is usually chipper
and filled with joy.

3

But today I feel startled,
confused, and perplexed.

I have a few questions
I cannot put to rest.

Please listen! Believe me!
I don't understand,

what seems to be happening
in this glorious land.

I've noticed some people
are not getting along.

I've heard them all
singing a different song.

It seems they've forgotten
how precious they are.

It seems that somehow...
this has gone too far.

look at this illusion take a picture unmindfulness for all to see

I will wrap myself up in
my blanket...and wait.

For the magical world good
folks will create.

A world of kindness,
compassion, and care.

care for humanity, with
one vision to share.

9

Mother says, "Oren, please
put your blanket away,

the world cannot change
in only one day."

I say, "change is too slow,
and mistakes they repeat!

Truth and sincerity are
replaced with deceit!

How long will this change
take to complete?"

10

11

Perhaps we should wonder,
and together let's ponder.

Let's change our pace,

since I truly believe
it is such a disgrace,

how some people treat others
in this magnificent place!

I will lift up my blanket
and look to the sky.

I will have hope,
and I will not cry.

For the many pure
blessings for which I yearn,

are found in nature. . .
and people must learn!

Behold! Mother Nature,
so glorious and grand!

Always so willing
to lend us a hand!

I await the comfortable
warmth of the sun,

that lets our Earth know
when the day has begun.

17

The leaves in the wind
sing a beautiful song,

Held up by branches
and trunks so strong.

The fragrant flowers grow
so unique and with grace,

And they never have
difficulty sharing their space.

18

19

So why don't more humans
make an effort to care?

To care for each other,
to be kind and fair?

What about empathy,
or protecting a friend?

Can it be these are
only pretend?

Now I've sometimes heard
a kind word or two.

I've faintly heard a,
"how do you do?"

But those who are fair,
just lately seem rare.

And I do not want them
to be in despair!

I'm going to have to
make a demand!

I will find a way to make
people understand!

Since we are capable
of so much more,

This just will not do
in this marvellous land!

Emermarie

N
W E
S

23

I will go to the
magical Emermarie.

I will find the answer
amongst the breeze.

I've heard of great happenings
there, both wondrous and true.

This will be the
perfect thing to do!

24

Good morning to you and
good morning to all!

All of a sudden, I feel
quite small.

Oh magical forest,
so honest and real,

People need your touch
in order to heal.

25

Glorious forest,
so quiet and still,

please give them some
hope to lift up their will.

"Good morning Oren," sang a
mountain bluebird.

"I am glad to see you...
woeful truths I have heard.

You don't need to explain,
I have a clear view.

I have seen how they act, and there is
much to do!"

"The blanket you carry
that keeps you warm,

is the blanket we'll use
for the world to transform.

Lay it down flat, for in it will be,

some special ingredients
provided by me.

For a magical blanket it will become,

which we'll wrap around the
world when we're done!"

29

honesty virtuous happiness righteousness clarity reflection accountability social responsibility individuality creativeness mindfulness compassion patience

faith

innocence

sincerity

passion

uniqueness

clarity justice care courage simplicity hope

joy fragility growth

awareness fairness growth

integrity privacy humility

human dignity empathy kindness growth

31

"Now my friend,
the magic is done.

The world has
transformed for everyone.

Be sure to spread
the crucial news!

Be sure to tell them
they have started anew!"

33.

"Oren, we are depending on you.

Please tell the whole
world to start anew.

Help them to realize
what we know is true.

That any wrong doing
that someone will do,

takes a piece out of
their own dignity too."

"Oren, my friend, don't let them forget.

The world is now new... completely reset!

The world is now ready to begin, but a pure spirit must come from within.

What goodness do you think the people will bring?"

35

◆ FriesenPress

Suite 300 - 990 Fort St
Victoria, BC, V8V 3K2
Canada

www.friesenpress.com

ISBN
978-1-5255-1076-2 (Paperback)
978-1-5255-1077-9 (eBook)

1. POETRY

Distributed to the trade by The Ingram Book Company

CPSIA information can be obtained
at www.ICGtesting.com
Printed in the USA
LVOW05s1716120218
566157LV00041B/803/P

9 781525 510762